HOW TO

SELL ANYTHING TO ANYONE

A STEP-BY-STEP GUIDE TO FINANCIAL FREEDOM THROUGH SALES MAXIMIZATION

Larry Peters

TABLE OF CONTENT

INTRODUCTION

In a world where transactions fuel the economy, the art of selling stands as a pillar of human interaction, commerce, and progress. In this light, knowing how to sell is paramount. "How to Sell Anything to Anyone: A Step-by-Step Guide to Financial Freedom Through Sales Maximization" has been carefully put together to help the reader grow from knowing absolutely nothing about sales to skyrocketing his or her sales within a short period of time. Within these pages lies a roadmap to not just understanding the mechanics of sales but mastering its nuances to unlock the doors to financial liberation.

Understanding the Power of Sales

At its core, sales transcend mere transactions; it embodies the essence of human connection. It's about more than just persuading someone to part with their hard-earned money; it's about understanding their needs, desires, and aspirations. Sales are the conduit through which solutions are offered, problems are solved, and relationships are forged. It's an intricate dance of communication, negotiation, and empathy that underpins the fabric of society.

Throughout history, those who have harnessed the power of sales have left an indelible mark on the world. From the charismatic merchants of ancient marketplaces to the visionary entrepreneurs of modern times, the ability to sell has been a catalyst for change, innovation, and progress. It's the driving force behind thriving businesses, burgeoning industries, and economic prosperity.

Why Selling is Essential for Financial Freedom

In today's dynamic economic landscape, financial freedom is no longer a distant dream but an attainable reality for those who understand the value of sales. Gone are the days when traditional career paths were the only route to financial stability. The rise of entrepreneurship, remote work, and the gig economy has ushered in a new era of opportunity where individuals have the autonomy to chart their own course to success.

At the heart of this entrepreneurial revolution lies the ability to sell. Whether you're launching a startup, freelancing as a consultant, or monetizing your passion project, the principles of effective sales are indispensable. Selling isn't just about making a sale; it's about creating value, building relationships, and fostering trust. It's about positioning yourself as a solution provider and a trusted advisor in the eyes of your customers.

In this book, we'll explore the multifaceted world of sales, equipping you with the tools, techniques, and strategies you need to thrive in any market environment. From mastering the mindset of a successful salesperson to leveraging technology and social media to amplify your reach, each chapter will provide actionable insights and practical guidance to help you maximize your sales potential.

So, whether you're an aspiring entrepreneur, a seasoned sales professional, or someone simply looking to enhance their financial prospects, "How to Sell Anything to Anyone" will serve as your indispensable companion on the journey to financial freedom. Are you ready to unlock the transformative power of sales and take control of your financial destiny? If so, let's embark on this journey together and discover the boundless opportunities that await.

CHAPTER ONE

MASTERING THE MINDSET OF A SUCCESSFUL SALESPERSON

The psychology of selling

Understanding the psychology of selling is akin to unlocking the secret code to influence, persuasion, and ultimately, success in sales. At the heart of the psychology of selling lies a deep understanding of human behavior. Every purchasing decision is driven by a complex interplay of emotions, desires, and motivations. By studying human behavior, sales professionals can gain valuable insights into what drives their customers, enabling them to tailor their approach and communication style accordingly.

From the principles of social proof and reciprocity to the psychology of scarcity and urgency, there are numerous psychological factors at play in the sales process. By understanding these principles, sales professionals can leverage them to influence customer behavior and drive sales. Let's examine some of them.

1. Building rapport and trust

Building rapport and trust is essential in sales, as it lays the foundation for successful relationships with customers. People are more likely to buy from those they know, like, and trust. By employing techniques such as active listening, mirroring body language, and finding common ground, sales professionals can establish rapport with their customers and create a sense of connection.

Trust is equally important in the sales process. Customers are more likely to make a purchase when they trust the salesperson and believe that the product or service will deliver on its promises. By being transparent, honest, and reliable, sales professionals can build trust with their customers and increase the likelihood of closing the sale.

2. Understanding Customer Needs and Pain Points

Effective selling begins with understanding the needs and pain points of the customer. By empathizing with the customer's situation and demonstrating an understanding of their challenges, sales professionals can position themselves as trusted advisors and solution providers.

One effective technique for understanding customer needs is active listening. By listening attentively to the customer's concerns and asking probing questions, sales professionals can uncover valuable insights that can inform their sales strategy.

3. Influencing Decision-Making Processes

The psychology of selling also involves understanding the factors that influence decision-making processes. People are often swayed by factors such as social proof, authority, and scarcity when making purchasing decisions. By leveraging these principles, sales professionals can influence customer behavior and increase their chances of making a sale.

For example, offering social proof in the form of customer testimonials or case studies can help reassure customers that they are making the right decision. Similarly, demonstrating authority and expertise in the field can instill confidence in the customer's mind.

4. Overcoming Objections

Finally, understanding the psychology of selling involves knowing how to overcome objections effectively. Objections are a natural part of the sales process, and sales professionals must be prepared to address them head-on.

One effective technique for overcoming objections is reframing them as opportunities. Instead of viewing objections as obstacles, sales professionals can reframe them as opportunities to address the customer's concerns and provide additional value.

By understanding human behavior, building rapport and trust, understanding customer needs, influencing decision-making processes, and overcoming objections, sales professionals can increase their effectiveness and achieve greater success in sales.

Understanding Limiting Beliefs

In the journey toward sales mastery and financial freedom, one of the most formidable obstacles that individuals encounter is the presence of limiting beliefs. These are deeply ingrained thoughts, perceptions, and self-imposed barriers that hinder progress, sabotage efforts, and impede success. It is important that we explore the nature of limiting beliefs, their impact on sales performance, and practical strategies for overcoming them to unleash your full potential as a successful salesperson.

Limiting beliefs are often formed early in life, influenced by past experiences, societal norms, and personal insecurities. They manifest as self-doubt, fear of failure, imposter syndrome, and a host of other negative thought patterns that undermine confidence and prevent individuals from reaching their goals.

In the context of sales, limiting beliefs can manifest in various ways. For example, a salesperson may believe they are not worthy of success, fear rejection or failure, or doubt their ability to persuade others effectively. These beliefs create mental barriers that impede performance, limit opportunities, and hinder progress in the sales journey.

Steps to Overcoming Limiting Beliefs

1. Identifying Limiting Beliefs

The first step in overcoming limiting beliefs is to identify and acknowledge their presence. This requires introspection and self-awareness to recognize the negative thought patterns and self-talk that are holding you back. Common signs of limiting beliefs include feelings of anxiety, self-criticism, and reluctance to take action.

To identify limiting beliefs, it can be helpful to keep a journal and record your thoughts and emotions as they arise throughout the day. Pay attention to recurring themes or patterns, and examine how these beliefs influence your behavior and decision-making in sales situations.

2. Challenging Limiting Beliefs

Once you've identified your limiting beliefs, the next step is to challenge them and replace them with more empowering beliefs. This requires a willingness to question the validity of your beliefs and challenge the assumptions underlying them.

One effective technique for challenging limiting beliefs is cognitive restructuring. This involves examining the evidence for and against the belief, reframing negative thoughts in a more positive light, and adopting a growth mindset focused on learning and improvement.

For example, if you believe you are not capable of closing big deals because you lack experience, challenge this belief by recalling past successes, seeking out mentors or role models who have achieved similar goals, and focusing on building your skills and expertise in sales.

3. Adopting Empowering Beliefs

Once you've challenged your limiting beliefs, the final step is to adopt empowering beliefs that support your goals and aspirations in sales. This involves cultivating a mindset of abundance, resilience, and self-confidence that enables you to overcome obstacles and seize opportunities with confidence.

Empowering beliefs may include beliefs such as "I am capable of achieving my sales goals," "Rejection is not personal and does not define my worth," and "Every setback is an opportunity for growth and learning."

By consciously adopting empowering beliefs and reinforcing them through positive affirmations, visualization, and goal-setting, you can reshape your mindset and unlock your full potential as a successful salesperson.

Conclusively, overcoming limiting beliefs is a critical step on the path to sales mastery and financial freedom. By identifying, challenging, and replacing negative beliefs with empowering ones, you can break free from the mental barriers that hold you back and unleash your full potential as a successful salesperson. Remember, your beliefs shape your reality—choose empowering beliefs that support your goals and aspirations, and watch as your sales performance and success soar to new heights.

Cultivating confidence and resilience

In the fast-paced and often unpredictable world of sales, cultivating confidence and resilience is not just advantageous—it's essential. Confidence empowers sales professionals to present themselves and their offerings with conviction, while resilience enables them to bounce back from setbacks and persevere in the face of challenges. In this light, we shall explore the importance of confidence and resilience in sales, practical strategies for cultivating these qualities, and their transformative impact on sales performance and overall success.

The Importance of Confidence

Confidence is the cornerstone of success in sales. It is a belief in oneself, one's abilities, and the value of what one has to offer. Confident sales professionals exude credibility, authority, and trustworthiness, which instills confidence in their customers and inspires them to take action.

Confidence enables sales professionals to approach prospects with ease, communicate persuasively, and handle objections with grace. It empowers them to navigate challenging situations, overcome rejection, and maintain a positive outlook even in the face of adversity.

Strategies for cultivating confidence

Confidence is not something that is innate—it can be cultivated and nurtured over time. One effective strategy for building confidence is to focus on strengths and successes. Reflecting on past achievements and recognizing one's abilities can boost self-esteem and instill a sense of confidence in one's capabilities.

Visualization is another powerful technique for cultivating confidence. By mentally rehearsing successful outcomes and envisioning oneself achieving goals, sales professionals can build confidence and reduce anxiety in high-pressure situations.

Additionally, setting realistic goals and celebrating small victories along the way can bolster confidence and reinforce a sense of accomplishment.

The importance of resilience

Resilience is the ability to bounce back from setbacks, adapt to change, and persevere in the face of adversity. In sales, resilience is crucial, as rejection, failure, and obstacles are inevitable aspects of the job.

Resilient sales professionals view setbacks as opportunities for growth and learning rather than insurmountable obstacles. They possess a mindset of perseverance and determination, refusing to be discouraged by temporary setbacks or challenges.

Strategies for cultivating resilience

Building resilience requires developing coping mechanisms and strategies for managing stress and adversity. One effective technique is to reframe challenges as opportunities for growth. By adopting a growth mindset and viewing setbacks as learning experiences, sales professionals can bounce back stronger and more resiliently than before.

Maintaining a healthy work-life balance is also essential for building resilience. Taking time to recharge, engage in hobbies, and nurture personal relationships can help prevent burnout and enhance overall resilience.

Additionally, cultivating a support network of mentors, colleagues, and friends can provide invaluable emotional support and encouragement during difficult times.

Confidence and resilience are indispensable qualities for success in sales. By cultivating confidence, sales professionals can approach their work with conviction, communicate persuasively, and inspire trust in their customers. Similarly, by fostering resilience, they can bounce back from setbacks, adapt to change, and persevere in the face of adversity.

By implementing the strategies outlined herein and committing to continuous growth and development, sales professionals can cultivate confidence and resilience and unlock their full potential for success in sales and beyond. Remember, confidence and resilience are not static traits—they are skills that can be developed and strengthened over time with dedication, effort, and perseverance.

Practical Guide: Mindset Exercises for Sales Success

In this practical guide, we'll explore a series of mindset exercises designed to help you internalize and practice the key concepts covered in the chapters on the psychology of selling, overcoming limiting beliefs, and cultivating confidence and resilience. By incorporating these exercises into your daily routine, you'll develop the mindset of a successful salesperson and enhance your ability to achieve sales success and financial freedom.

1. Daily Affirmations

Start each day with a series of positive affirmations that reinforce your confidence, resilience, and belief in your ability to succeed in sales. Write down affirmations such as "I am confident in my sales abilities," "I am resilient in the face of challenges," and "I attract success and abundance in my sales endeavors." Repeat these affirmations aloud or silently to yourself several times each morning to set a positive tone for the day ahead.

2. Visualization Exercises

Take a few moments each day to visualize yourself achieving your sales goals and overcoming challenges with ease. Close your eyes and imagine yourself confidently approaching prospects, delivering persuasive sales pitches, and closing deals with finesse. Visualize the emotions you'll experience when you achieve success, such as joy, pride, and satisfaction. Use all of your senses to make the visualization as vivid and realistic as possible.

3. Reframing Limiting Beliefs

Identify one of your limiting beliefs related to sales, such as "I'm not good enough to succeed" or "I'm afraid of rejection." Write down this belief on a piece of paper, then challenge it by reframing it in a more positive light. For example, reframe "I'm not good enough" as "I have unique skills and strengths that make me a valuable asset in sales." Keep this reframed belief somewhere visible, such as on your desk or bathroom mirror, and repeat it to yourself whenever the limiting belief resurfaces.

4. Goal-Setting and Action Planning

Set specific, measurable sales goals for yourself, such as the number of new leads to generate, the amount of revenue to generate, or the number of sales calls to make each week. Break down these goals into smaller, actionable steps, and create a detailed action plan for achieving them. Schedule specific times each day or week to work on these action steps, and hold yourself accountable for following through.

5. Journaling and Reflection

Take time each day to journal about your experiences in sales, including successes, challenges, and lessons learned. Write down any limiting beliefs or negative thoughts that arise, and challenge them by reframing them in a more positive light. Reflect on your progress toward your sales goals, celebrate your achievements, and identify areas for improvement. Regular journaling can help you track your growth and development over time and reinforce a positive mindset.

6. Seeking support and feedback

Don't hesitate to reach out to mentors, colleagues, or friends for support and feedback on your sales journey. Share your goals, challenges, and successes with them, and ask for their insights and advice. Seek constructive feedback on your sales pitches, strategies, and approaches, and be open to incorporating their suggestions into your practice. Surrounding yourself with a supportive network of people who believe in your abilities can provide invaluable encouragement and motivation.

Incorporate these mindset exercises into your daily routine to cultivate the confidence, resilience, and positive mindset necessary for sales success. Remember that mindset is a skill that can be developed and strengthened over time with practice and persistence. By committing to regular practice and reflection, you'll enhance your sales performance, overcome limiting beliefs, and unlock your full potential as a successful salesperson on the path to financial freedom.

CHAPTER TWO

KNOWING YOUR PRODUCT INSIDE OUT

Knowing your product inside out is crucial to being able to sell anything to anyone. Having comprehensive product knowledge is important for sales success. It is necessary to understand every aspect of the product or service being sold, from its features and benefits to its applications and value proposition. Having in-depth product knowledge builds credibility and trust with customers, enables effective communication of value, and allows sales professionals to tailor their pitch to meet the specific needs and preferences of potential buyers.

This chapter is aimed at helping the reader discover practical strategies for acquiring and retaining product knowledge, including conducting thorough research, engaging with product experts, and leveraging training resources provided by the company. By mastering the ins and outs of their product or service, sales professionals can position themselves as trusted advisors and maximize their effectiveness in persuading customers to make a purchase.

Product Knowledge: The Key to Building Trust

In the expansive realm of sales, where persuasion meets opportunity, one indispensable asset stands out above all: comprehensive product knowledge. Let us delve into the pivotal role that product knowledge plays in building trust—a cornerstone of successful salesmanship.

1. Establishing Credibility

Credibility is the currency of sales. Customers are more likely to trust and engage with sales professionals who demonstrate a thorough understanding of what they're selling. When you possess in-depth product knowledge, you exude confidence and authority, positioning yourself as a trustworthy expert in your field. This credibility is the foundation upon which successful sales relationships are built.

2. Fostering Trust

Trust is the linchpin of any successful sales interaction. When customers perceive that you have a genuine grasp of your product or service, they are more inclined to trust your recommendations and guidance. Comprehensive product knowledge demonstrates your commitment to understanding and meeting the needs of your customers, fostering trust and confidence in your ability to deliver value.

3. Communicating value effectively

The ability to articulate the value of your product or service is essential in sales. Comprehensive product knowledge enables you to effectively communicate the features, benefits, and unique selling points that set your offering apart from the competition. By highlighting how your product or service addresses the specific needs and challenges of your customers, you can make a compelling case for its value, increasing the likelihood of a successful sale.

4. Building long-term relationships

Sales success extends far beyond individual transactions—it lies in building long-term, mutually beneficial relationships with customers. When you demonstrate a deep understanding of your product or service and consistently deliver value, you foster loyalty and trust among your customer base. These enduring relationships not only lead to repeat business but also serve as a foundation for referrals and advocacy, driving sustained growth and success.

5. Continuous learning and improvement

In the dynamic landscape of sales, product knowledge is not static—it requires continuous learning and improvement. Stay abreast of updates, enhancements, and industry trends related to your product or service. Invest time in training, workshops, and educational resources to deepen your understanding and refine your expertise. By embracing a mindset of lifelong learning, you ensure that your product knowledge remains relevant and impactful, fueling your success in sales.

Product knowledge is the cornerstone of sales mastery. By investing in a deep understanding of your product or service, you lay the groundwork for building trust, communicating value, and fostering long-term relationships with customers. Armed with comprehensive product knowledge, you possess the key to unlocking sales success and achieving financial freedom in the competitive world of sales.

Understanding Customer Needs and Pain Points

In order to gain comprehensive product knowledge so as to be able to sell anything to anyone, one of the pivotal aspects to put into consideration is the critical importance of understanding customer needs and pain points. Comprehensive product knowledge isn't just about knowing your own offering; it's also about understanding how it meets the needs and addresses the pain points of your potential customers. It incorporates empathizing with customers, uncovering their challenges, and offering tailored solutions that can elevate your sales game and drive financial success. Understanding customer needs and pain points can be achieved through:

1. Empathizing with Customers

Successful salesmanship begins with empathy. Understanding the challenges, aspirations, and pain points of your customers is essential for building rapport and trust. By putting yourself in their shoes, you can gain valuable insights into their motivations and priorities, enabling you to tailor your sales approach to meet their specific needs.

2. Uncovering customer needs

Effective selling is not about pushing a product or service onto unwilling customers; it's about identifying and addressing genuine needs and desires. By asking probing questions and actively listening to your customers, you can uncover their underlying needs, preferences, and pain points. This information serves as the foundation for crafting personalized solutions that resonate with their unique circumstances.

3. Addressing pain points

Every customer has pain points—challenges, frustrations, or problems they are seeking to overcome. By identifying and addressing these pain points head-on, you can position your product or service as the solution they've been searching for. Whether it's saving time, reducing costs, or improving efficiency, understanding and empathizing with your customers' pain points allows you to offer compelling solutions that meet their needs and add value.

4. Tailoring Solutions

One size does not fit all in sales. A cookie-cutter approach may yield limited results, as each customer has unique needs and preferences. By leveraging your comprehensive product knowledge and understanding of customer needs, you can tailor your sales pitch to resonate with each individual customer. Whether it's highlighting specific features or benefits that address their pain points or customizing pricing and packaging options, personalization is key to driving customer satisfaction and closing sales.

5. Building trust and loyalty

When customers feel understood and valued, they are more likely to trust and remain loyal to your brand. By demonstrating a genuine interest in their needs, actively listening to their concerns, and offering tailored solutions, you establish yourself as a trusted advisor and partner in their success. This trust and loyalty pave the way for long-term relationships, repeat business, and referrals, driving sustained growth and profitability.

By and large, understanding customer needs and pain points is a foundational element of successful selling. By empathizing with customers, uncovering their challenges, addressing their pain points, and tailoring solutions to meet their needs, you can build trust, drive sales, and achieve financial freedom in the competitive world of sales.

Communicating value effectively

Knowing your product or service inside out isn't just about possessing knowledge; it's about effectively communicating the value it offers to potential customers. This section highlights the importance of articulating the benefits, features, and unique selling points of your offering in a compelling manner that resonates with your audience. It is paramount to cultivate strategies for crafting persuasive sales pitches, addressing customer concerns, and ultimately driving sales by effectively communicating the value of your product or service. The following steps have been outlined to enable you to communicate your product's value effectively.

1. Highlighting Features and Benefits

Effective communication of value begins with a clear understanding of the features and benefits of your product or service. Features are the specific characteristics or functionalities of your offering, while benefits are the advantages or outcomes that customers derive from using it. By highlighting how these features translate into tangible benefits that address customer needs or pain points, you can effectively communicate the value proposition of your product or service.

2. Tailoring the message

Not all customers have the same needs or priorities. To effectively communicate value, it's essential to tailor your message to resonate with the specific concerns and preferences of your audience. Consider the unique challenges or pain points your customers face and emphasize how your product or service provides a solution or meets their specific needs. By customizing your pitch to address the individual concerns of each customer, you can increase the relevance and impact of your message.

3. Using Stories and Examples

Stories are a powerful tool for illustrating the value of your product or service in a relatable and memorable way. Share success stories, case studies, or testimonials that demonstrate how your offering has helped other customers overcome challenges or achieve their goals. Use concrete examples and real-world scenarios to paint a vivid picture of the benefits and outcomes that customers can expect, making your value proposition more tangible and compelling.

4. Addressing Objections

Effective communication of value also involves addressing customer objections or concerns head-on. Anticipate common objections that customers may raise, such as price, quality, or suitability, and prepare persuasive responses that alleviate their concerns. Use your comprehensive product knowledge to provide evidence-based explanations and solutions that demonstrate the value and credibility of your offering.

5. Creating visual aids

Visual aids can enhance the clarity and impact of your message when communicating value. Use charts, graphs, demonstrations, or multimedia presentations to illustrate key points, showcase product features, or provide visual evidence of the benefits of your offering. Visual aids can help capture the attention of your audience, reinforce your message, and leave a lasting impression that enhances their understanding and appreciation of the value you offer.

Practical Guide for Product Knowledge Checklist and Practice Scenarios

In this practical guide, we'll provide a checklist and practice scenarios to help you internalize and apply the principles discussed on product knowledge, understanding customer needs and pain points, and communicating value effectively. By utilizing this guide, you'll be able to strengthen your product knowledge, enhance your understanding of customer needs, and sharpen your skills in effectively communicating the value of your offering.

1. Product Knowledge Checklist

Use the following checklist to ensure that you have a comprehensive understanding of your product or service:

Familiarize yourself with all the features and functionalities of the product or service.

Understand how each feature translates into tangible benefits for the customer.

Be aware of any potential limitations or drawbacks of the product or service.

Research competitor products or services to identify points of differentiation.

Stay updated on any updates, enhancements, or changes to the product or service.

2. Practice Scenarios

Engage in the following practice scenarios to reinforce your product knowledge and sharpen your sales skills:

Scenario 1: Role-playing customer interactions

Partner with a colleague or friend to role-play different customer interactions.

Practice explaining the features and benefits of your product or service in response to common customer questions or objections.

Experiment with different communication techniques and approaches to effectively convey the value proposition of your offering.

Scenario 2: Customer Needs Assessment

Create hypothetical customer profiles representing various demographics and industries.

Identify the specific needs, pain points, and priorities of each customer profile.

Practice tailoring your sales pitch to address the unique concerns and preferences of each customer segment.

Scenario 3: Value Proposition Presentation

Develop a compelling value proposition presentation highlighting the key features, benefits, and value proposition of your product or service.

Practice delivering this presentation to a colleague, friend, or mentor, seeking feedback on clarity, effectiveness, and persuasiveness.

Iterate and refine your presentation based on feedback to enhance its impact.

3. Reflection and Feedback:

After completing each practice scenario, take time to reflect on your performance and seek feedback from others. Consider the following questions:

What aspects of the interaction went well? What areas could be improved?

Did you effectively communicate the value proposition of your product or service?

Were you able to address customer needs and concerns adequately?

What strategies or techniques were most effective in conveying value and building trust?

CHAPTER THREE

DEVELOPING EFFECTIVE SALES TECHNIQUES

"Developing Effective Sales Techniques" in "How to Sell Anything to Anyone" entails mastering the skills necessary to connect with customers, understand their needs, and influence their purchasing decisions. It entails building rapport, asking insightful questions, active listening, presenting solutions, handling objections, and closing sales. Effective sales techniques can be developed through:

Building rapport and trust

Building rapport and trust with customers is an essential aspect of successful salesmanship. It encompasses establishing genuine connections, fostering trust, and creating a positive rapport with customers to drive sales and achieve financial freedom. Let us delve into the strategies and techniques that cultivate rapport, build trust, and lay the groundwork for fruitful sales interactions and lasting relationships.

1. Authentic Connection

Building rapport begins with establishing an authentic connection with customers. Sales professionals must approach interactions with sincerity, empathy, and a genuine interest in understanding the needs and preferences of their customers. By demonstrating authenticity and warmth, sales professionals can create a welcoming atmosphere that encourages open communication and fosters trust.

2. Active Listening

Active listening is a fundamental skill in building rapport and trust. Sales professionals must listen attentively to their customers, paying close attention to verbal and nonverbal cues and seeking to understand their perspectives fully. By demonstrating genuine interest and empathy, sales professionals can show customers that their concerns and preferences are valued, fostering a sense of trust and rapport.

3. Finding common ground

Finding common ground with customers helps to establish a sense of connection and mutual understanding. Sales professionals can identify shared interests, experiences, or values that resonate with their customers and use them as a basis for building rapport. By highlighting shared experiences or perspectives, sales professionals can create a sense of camaraderie and rapport that strengthens the bond between themselves and their customers.

4. Building Credibility

Credibility is essential for establishing trust with customers. Sales professionals must demonstrate expertise, reliability, and integrity in their interactions to instill confidence in their recommendations and advice. By providing accurate information, delivering on promises, and acting with honesty and transparency, sales professionals can build credibility and trust with customers, laying the foundation for successful sales relationships.

5. Empathy and understanding

Empathy is a powerful tool for building rapport and trust. Sales professionals must put themselves in their customers' shoes, understanding their needs, concerns, and challenges from their perspective. By demonstrating empathy and understanding, sales professionals can show customers that they are genuinely invested in helping them find the right solution to their needs, fostering trust and confidence in their expertise.

6. Consistency and reliability

Consistency and reliability are key components of trust-building in sales. Sales professionals must consistently deliver on their promises, follow through on commitments, and provide reliable support and service to their customers. By demonstrating consistency and reliability in their actions, sales professionals can build trust and confidence with customers over time, leading to long-term relationships and repeat business.

Asking powerful questions

After rapport and trust have been built, the art of asking powerful questions takes center stage as a pivotal skill for sales success. This entails the art of asking insightful and thought-provoking questions to uncover customer needs, understand their pain points, and guide them toward a solution that meets their unique requirements. This section highlights the strategies and techniques for asking powerful questions that elicit valuable information and drive meaningful sales conversations, ultimately leading to financial freedom through sales maximization.

1. Probing for Needs and Pain Points

Asking powerful questions involves probing beyond surface-level inquiries to uncover the underlying needs, desires, and pain points of customers. Sales professionals must delve deep into the motivations and challenges of their customers by asking open-ended questions that encourage reflection and exploration. By probing for needs and pain points, sales professionals can gain valuable insights that inform their sales approach and enable them to offer tailored solutions.

2. Active listening and empathy

Effective questioning goes hand in hand with active listening and empathy. Sales professionals must listen attentively to their customers' responses, paying close attention to both verbal and nonverbal cues and demonstrating empathy for their concerns and challenges. By showing genuine interest and understanding, sales professionals can create a supportive environment that encourages customers to open up and share valuable insights.

3. Uncovering Motivations and Goals

Powerful questions are aimed at uncovering the motivations, goals, and aspirations of customers. Sales professionals must inquire about the desired outcomes and objectives that customers hope to achieve, as well as the challenges or obstacles standing in their way. By understanding customers' motivations and goals, sales professionals can tailor their sales pitch to align with their aspirations and offer solutions that address their specific needs.

4. Challenging Assumptions and Perspectives

Asking powerful questions involves challenging assumptions and perspectives to encourage critical thinking and exploration. Sales professionals must not shy away from asking tough or thought-provoking questions that challenge customers' preconceived notions or beliefs. By prompting customers to reconsider their perspectives and assumptions, sales professionals can uncover new opportunities and perspectives that may lead to innovative solutions.

5. Guiding the sales conversation

Powerful questions serve as a guide for navigating the sales conversation and steering it toward a mutually beneficial outcome. Sales professionals must use questions strategically to lead customers through the sales process, addressing concerns, overcoming objections, and highlighting the value proposition of their offering. By guiding the conversation with powerful questions, sales professionals can maintain control and momentum, ultimately leading to a successful sale.

6. Building trust and rapport

Asking powerful questions shouldn't end with gathering information; it should also include building trust and rapport with customers. Sales professionals must approach questioning with sincerity, empathy, and a genuine desire to understand and help their customers. By demonstrating a genuine interest in their needs and concerns, sales professionals can build trust and credibility, laying the foundation for a successful sales relationship.

Techniques for closing the deal

Mastering the techniques for closing the deal is paramount for achieving sales success and financial freedom. Here are several techniques for closing the deal:

1. Trial Close

The trial close involves asking a series of questions or making statements to gauge the customer's readiness to buy. By subtly prompting the customer to make a decision or express interest, sales professionals can assess the customer's readiness to move forward with the purchase.

2. Assumptive Close

The assumptive close involves assuming that the customer has already decided to make the purchase and proceeding with the next steps accordingly. By confidently guiding the customer through the closing process as if the decision has already been made, sales professionals can encourage a positive response and expedite the sales process.

3. Alternative Choice Close

The alternative choice close involves presenting the customer with two or more options, all of which lead to a positive outcome for the sales professional. By offering the customer multiple choices, sales professionals can empower them to make a decision while subtly steering them toward a favorable outcome for the sale.

4. Urgency Close

The urgency close involves creating a sense of urgency or scarcity to motivate the customer to make a decision quickly. By highlighting limited-time offers, special promotions, or impending price increases, sales professionals can encourage customers to act promptly to secure the best deal.

5. Summary Close

The summary close involves summarizing the key points of the sales conversation and reaffirming the value proposition before asking for the sale. By recapping the benefits and features of the product or service and reaffirming its value, sales professionals can reinforce the customer's decision-making process and prompt them to finalize the purchase.

6. Silent Close

The silent close involves remaining silent after presenting the sales pitch or asking for the sale, allowing the customer to respond without interruption. By giving the customer space to consider the offer and make a decision without pressure, sales professionals can encourage them to take ownership of the decision and commit to the purchase.

7. Negotiation Close

The negotiation process involves negotiating terms or concessions with the customer to overcome any remaining objections and finalize the sale. By engaging in a collaborative dialogue with the customer and addressing any remaining concerns or objections, sales professionals can reach a mutually beneficial agreement and close the deal.

Each of these closing techniques serves a unique purpose and can be adapted to suit the preferences and personalities of both the sales professional and the customer. By mastering these techniques and incorporating them into their sales approach, sales professionals can increase their effectiveness in closing deals and achieve financial freedom through sales maximization.

Practical Guide for Role-Playing Exercises for Sales Techniques

Carry out the following exercises, which have been designed to help you develop confidence, sharpen your skills, and enhance your effectiveness in sales interactions, ultimately leading you toward financial freedom through sales maximization.

1. Building rapport and trust

Role-Playing Scenario:

Pair up with a colleague, friend, or family member.

Take turns playing the roles of the sales professional and the customer.

Practice initiating the sales conversation, establishing rapport, and building trust through active listening, empathy, and authentic communication.

Experiment with different approaches and techniques for building rapport and trust, such as finding common ground, mirroring body language, and demonstrating credibility.

2. Asking powerful questions

Role-Playing Scenario:

Role-play various customer scenarios, such as a first-time buyer, a hesitant prospect, or a skeptical customer.

Practice asking open-ended questions that encourage customers to share their needs, preferences, and pain points.

Experiment with probing questions that delve deeper into specific areas of interest or concern, uncovering valuable insights and driving meaningful conversations.

Focus on active listening and empathy, responding thoughtfully to the customer's responses, and demonstrating genuine interest in their perspective.

3. Closing the Deal: Techniques and Strategies

Role-Playing Scenario:

Role-play different closing techniques and strategies, such as the trial close, assumptive close, or urgency close.

Practice guiding the sales conversation toward a mutually beneficial outcome, addressing any remaining concerns or objections along the way.

Experiment with different closing approaches to see which ones resonate most effectively with your style and personality.

Focus on maintaining confidence and composure throughout the closing process, remaining open to negotiation, and being flexible in your approach.

By engaging in these role-playing exercises, you will have the opportunity to internalize and practice the key techniques outlined for building rapport and trust, asking powerful questions, and closing the deal. Remember to approach each exercise with an open mind, a willingness to learn, and a commitment to continuous improvement. Mastery of these skills is essential for achieving financial freedom through sales maximization.

CHAPTER FOUR

THE POWER OF LEVERAGING TECHNOLOGY AND SOCIAL MEDIA IN SALES

In order to be able to sell anything to anyone, a professional seller must recognize the transformative impact of technology and social media on the sales landscape. He or she must explore and harness the power of technology and leverage social media platforms, through which one can revolutionize sales strategies, expand reach, and drive unparalleled growth in sales revenue. Below are the key ways in which technology and social media can be utilized to optimize sales processes and maximize financial freedom.

1. Expanding Reach and Visibility

Social media platforms such as Facebook, Instagram, LinkedIn, and Twitter offer unprecedented opportunities to reach a vast audience of potential customers. By establishing a strong presence on these platforms through organic content, sales professionals can increase brand visibility, expand their reach, and connect with prospects from around the globe.

2. Building Relationships and Trust

Social media provides a platform for building authentic relationships with customers through engagement, interaction, and personalized communication. Sales professionals can use social media to engage with prospects, provide valuable content, and address customer inquiries, thereby nurturing trust and credibility over time.

3. Targeted marketing and advertising

Technology enables precise targeting of marketing and advertising efforts, allowing sales professionals to reach specific demographics, interests, and behaviors. Through data analytics and insights, sales professionals can identify and target high-potential prospects with tailored messages and offers, maximizing the effectiveness of their marketing campaigns.

4. Streamlining sales processes

Technology offers a range of tools and platforms designed to streamline sales processes, automate repetitive tasks, and increase efficiency. Sales professionals can leverage customer relationship management (CRM) software, email automation tools, and sales analytics platforms to manage leads, track interactions, and optimize sales performance.

5. Enhancing the customer experience

Technology enables personalized, data-driven customer experiences that cater to individual preferences and needs. Through tools such as chatbots, personalized messaging, and dynamic content, sales professionals can deliver tailored solutions and recommendations that resonate with customers, enhancing satisfaction and loyalty.

6. Monitoring and Measuring Performance

Technology provides valuable insights and analytics that enable sales professionals to monitor and measure performance effectively. By tracking key performance indicators (KPIs), analyzing sales data, and identifying trends, sales professionals can make informed decisions, iterate on strategies, and drive continuous improvement in sales performance.

Utilizing social media platforms for outreach

Social media platforms have a profound impact on modern sales strategies. The sales professional must strategically utilize social media for outreach purposes and explore how he or she can leverage these platforms to expand the market reach, engage with prospects, and drive sales growth. Now, let us comprehensively explore the key strategies and techniques for effectively utilizing social media platforms for outreach and sales.

1. Establishing a Strong Presence

Building a robust presence on social media platforms is essential for successful outreach. Sales professionals should create professional profiles on platforms such as LinkedIn, Facebook, Instagram, Twitter, and others relevant to their target audience.

Profiles should be optimized with compelling visuals, informative content, and clear messaging that highlights the value proposition of the sales professional and their offerings.

2. Identifying and Targeting the Right Audience

Social media platforms offer powerful targeting capabilities that allow sales professionals to reach specific demographics, interests, and behaviors. Utilize the platform's built-in analytics tools to identify and understand the characteristics of your target audience. This includes demographics, interests, online behaviors, and preferences.

3. Engaging with Content

Content is the most important thing in the realm of social media. Sales professionals should regularly share valuable content that educates, entertains, or inspires their audience.

Engage with your audience by posting updates, sharing industry news, offering tips and advice, and showcasing success stories. Encourage interaction through likes, comments, and shares to foster a sense of community and build relationships.

4. Leveraging Paid Advertising

Paid advertising on social media platforms provides a targeted and cost-effective way to reach a larger audience. Utilize paid advertising features such as sponsored posts, targeted ads, and promoted content to amplify your reach and target specific segments of your audience. Experiment with different ad formats, targeting options, and messaging to boost your campaigns for the best results.

5. Building Relationships through Networking

Social media platforms serve as virtual networking hubs where sales professionals can connect with prospects, industry peers, and thought leaders.

Actively engage in networking activities such as joining relevant groups and communities, participating in discussions, and attending virtual events. Establish genuine relationships by offering value, sharing insights, and providing support for your connections.

6. Analyzing Performance and Iterating Strategies

Monitor and analyze the performance of your social media outreach efforts using platform analytics and tracking tools.

Evaluate key metrics such as engagement rate, reach, click-through rate, and conversion rate to assess the effectiveness of your strategies. Use these insights to iterate and refine your approach, optimizing your outreach efforts for better results over time.

Email marketing strategies

Email marketing is a powerful tool for driving sales growth and maximizing financial freedom. There are different email marketing strategies that enable sales professionals to effectively reach, engage, and convert prospects into customers. The most important of these strategies are discussed below.

1. Building a Targeted Email List

The foundation of successful email marketing is a quality email list comprised of interested prospects and potential customers. Utilize various channels, including social media, website opt-ins, events, and networking, to capture email addresses from individuals who have expressed interest in your products or services.

2. Personalized and segmented campaigns

Personalization is key to engaging recipients and driving conversions. Segment your email list based on factors such as demographics, behavior, interests, and purchase history. Craft tailored messages and offers that resonate with each segment of your audience, addressing their specific needs, preferences, and pain points.

3. Compelling and value-driven content

Delivering valuable content is essential for keeping subscribers engaged and interested in your emails. Create compelling and relevant content, including informative articles, how-to guides, case studies, customer testimonials, and exclusive offers. Provide value with each email to establish credibility and build trust with your audience.

4. Engaging subject lines and email copy

The subject line is the first impression of your email and plays a crucial role in determining whether it gets opened or not. Craft attention-grabbing subject lines that are concise, compelling, and relevant to the recipient's interests. Keep the email copy clear, concise, and focused on the value proposition, avoiding jargon or overly salesy language.

5. Call-to-Action (CTA) Optimization

A strong and clear call-to-action (CTA) is essential for guiding recipients towards the desired action, whether it's making a purchase, signing up for a webinar, or downloading a resource. Place CTAs strategically within your email content, making them prominent, visually appealing, and compelling. Use actionable language that encourages immediate response, such as "Shop Now," "Learn More," or "Get Started."

6. Testing and Optimization

Continuously test and optimize your email campaigns to improve performance and maximize results. Experiment with different elements such as subject lines, email copy, CTAs, send times, and frequency to identify what resonates best with your audience. Use A/B testing to compare variations and determine the most effective strategies for driving engagement and conversions.

7. Compliance with Regulations and Best Practices

Ensure compliance with relevant regulations, such as the CAN-SPAM Act and GDPR, to maintain trust and credibility with your audience.

Adhere to best practices for email marketing, including obtaining explicit consent from subscribers, providing an easy opt-out option, and maintaining transparency in your email communications.

Leveraging CRM Systems for Effective Follow-Up

Customer Relationship Management (CRM) systems play a pivotal role in facilitating effective follow-up strategies. A strong grasp of CRM systems and their leverage enable sales professionals to organize, track, and manage customer interactions, enabling them to build stronger relationships, drive sales growth, and achieve financial freedom. Here, we comprehensively examine the key benefits and strategies for leveraging CRM systems for effective follow-up in sales.

1. Centralized Customer Data Management

CRM systems serve as centralized databases for storing and organizing customer data, including contact information, interactions, preferences, purchase history, and more.

Hint: Sales professionals can leverage CRM systems to access comprehensive profiles of their customers, enabling them to gain valuable insights, understand their needs, and tailor their follow-up strategies accordingly.

2. Automated follow-up processes

CRM systems offer automation capabilities that streamline and simplify the follow-up process, saving time and ensuring consistency.

Hint: Set up automated workflows and triggers to send personalized follow-up emails, reminders, and notifications based on predefined criteria such as lead status, interaction history, or specific actions taken by the customer.

3. Timely and targeted follow-up

CRM systems enable sales professionals to schedule follow-up activities and reminders, ensuring timely and proactive engagement with customers.

Hint: Leverage CRM tools to segment your customer database and prioritize follow-up efforts based on factors such as lead quality, purchase intent, or stage in the sales cycle. This allows you to focus your efforts on high-potential prospects and opportunities.

4. Personalized Communication

Personalization is key to effective follow-up. CRM systems provide the necessary data and tools to personalize follow-up communications based on the recipient's preferences, interests, and previous interactions.

Hint: Use merge tags and dynamic content to customize follow-up emails with the recipient's name, company, or other relevant information. Tailor your messaging to address specific needs or concerns identified through previous interactions.

5. Tracking and Monitoring

CRM systems offer robust tracking and monitoring capabilities that enable sales professionals to monitor the effectiveness of their follow-up efforts in real-time.

Hint: Track email opens, click-through rates, response rates, and other key metrics to gauge engagement and identify areas for improvement. Use this data to refine your follow-up strategies and optimize performance over time.

6. Integration with Other Tools and Platforms

CRM systems can integrate seamlessly with other tools and platforms, such as email marketing software, social media platforms, and productivity tools.

Hint: Integrate your CRM system with email marketing platforms to sync customer data and streamline communication. Utilize social media integrations to track customer interactions and engagement across multiple channels, allowing for more informed follow-up strategies.

7. Cultivating long-term relationships

Effective follow-up is essential for cultivating long-term relationships with customers and maximizing their lifetime value.

Hint: Use CRM systems to maintain ongoing communication with customers beyond the initial sale, nurturing relationships through regular check-ins, personalized offers, and value-added content. By staying engaged and responsive, you can build loyalty and trust over time, leading to repeat business and referrals.

Practical Guide for Creating a Social Media Sales Plan

Below is a practical guide that will walk you through the process of creating a comprehensive social media sales plan to effectively leverage social media platforms for outreach, integrate email marketing strategies, and utilize CRM systems for effective follow-up:

1. Define your objectives.

Start by clarifying your objectives and goals for social media sales. Are you looking to increase brand awareness, generate leads, drive website traffic, or directly increase sales? Define specific, measurable goals that align with your overall sales objectives.

2. Identify your target audience.

Understand your target audience and where they are most active on social media. Carry out research in order to identify their demographics, interests, behaviors, and preferences. This will help you tailor your social media strategy to effectively reach and engage with your ideal customers.

3. Choose the Right Social Media Platforms

Select the social media platforms that align best with your target audience and business objectives. Consider factors such as audience demographics, platform features, and content preferences. Focus your efforts on platforms where your audience is most likely to be active and engaged.

4. Develop a content strategy.

Create a content strategy that resonates with your target audience and supports your sales objectives. Determine the types of content you will create, such as blog posts, videos, infographics, or interactive content. Plan out a content calendar to ensure consistent and relevant posting.

5. Implement engagement tactics.

Engagement is key to building relationships and driving sales on social media. Develop tactics to encourage interaction and participation from your audience, such as asking questions, running polls or contests, hosting live Q&A sessions, and responding promptly to comments and messages.

6. Integrate email marketing.

Integrate email marketing into your social media sales plan to nurture leads and drive conversions. Use social media to capture email addresses through lead generation forms, contests, or gated content. Develop email campaigns that complement your social media content and provide additional value to subscribers.

7. Utilize CRM systems for follow-up.

Implement CRM systems to effectively follow up with leads and prospects generated through social media. Integrate social media lead data into your CRM system to track interactions, segment leads, and automate follow-up processes. Use CRM insights to personalize communication and drive conversions.

8. Set key performance indicators (KPIs).

Establish key performance indicators (KPIs) to measure the success of your social media sales plan. Track metrics such as reach, engagement, lead generation, conversion rate, and revenue generated. Regularly review and analyze performance data to identify areas for improvement and optimization.

9. Monitor and adjust your strategy.

Continuously monitor the performance of your social media sales plan and make adjustments as needed. Stay informed about changes in social media algorithms, audience behavior, and industry trends. Experiment with different tactics and strategies to optimize your approach and achieve your sales goals.

10.   Review and iterate.

Regularly review your social media sales plan to assess its effectiveness and impact on your sales objectives. Gather feedback from your team and stakeholders, and incorporate lessons learned into future iterations of your strategy. Stay agile and adaptive to evolving market conditions and customer needs.

CHAPTER FIVE

BUILDING AND MAINTAINING LONG-TERM RELATIONSHIPS

Building and maintaining long-term relationships in "How to Sell Anything to Anyone" emphasizes the importance of cultivating strong connections with customers beyond the initial sale. It involves consistently providing value, offering exceptional service, and demonstrating genuine care for customers' needs and satisfaction. By prioritizing long-term relationships, sales professionals can foster loyalty, earn repeat business, and secure valuable referrals, ultimately contributing to sustained sales growth and financial success.

The importance of customer relationship management

Building and maintaining long-term relationships emphasizes the critical importance of customer relationship management (CRM) for sales professionals aiming to foster long-term relationships with their clients. CRM goes beyond mere transactional interactions, focusing on nurturing connections, understanding customer needs, and delivering personalized experiences. Below is a comprehensive exploration of why CRM is vital for building enduring relationships and achieving sales maximization:

1. Enhanced Customer Understanding

CRM systems allow sales professionals to gather and organize comprehensive data about their customers, including contact information, purchase history, preferences, and interactions. By analyzing this data, sales professionals can gain valuable insights into customer behavior, preferences, and needs, enabling them to tailor their approach and communication to better serve their clients.

2. Personalized Communication

With CRM, sales professionals can personalize their communication and interactions with clients based on their unique preferences and past interactions. By addressing customers by name, referencing previous purchases or inquiries, and offering relevant recommendations, sales professionals can demonstrate that they understand and value their clients, fostering stronger connections and trust.

3. Timely follow-up and engagement

CRM systems enable sales professionals to schedule and automate follow-up activities, ensuring timely and consistent engagement with clients. Whether it's sending personalized emails, making follow-up calls, or scheduling appointments, CRM helps sales professionals stay organized and proactive in nurturing relationships with their clients, ultimately leading to higher customer satisfaction and loyalty.

4. Opportunity Identification

CRM systems can help sales professionals identify opportunities for upselling, cross-selling, or additional services based on customer behavior and preferences. By tracking purchase history, browsing patterns, and engagement levels, sales professionals can pinpoint opportunities to offer relevant products or services that meet their clients' evolving needs, driving revenue growth and maximizing customer lifetime value.

5. Efficient task management

CRM systems streamline task management and workflow processes, allowing sales professionals to stay organized and focused on building relationships with their clients. From setting reminders for follow-up calls to assigning tasks for team members, CRM helps ensure that no opportunity or interaction falls through the cracks, enabling sales professionals to provide consistent and reliable service to their clients.

6. Improved collaboration and coordination

CRM facilitates collaboration and coordination among sales teams, allowing them to share valuable insights, collaborate on strategies, and coordinate efforts to better serve their clients. By centralizing customer data and communication channels, CRM fosters a cohesive and aligned approach to relationship management, ultimately leading to more effective sales outcomes and customer satisfaction.

7. Long-Term Relationship Building

At its core, CRM is about nurturing long-term relationships with clients beyond individual transactions. By consistently delivering value, demonstrating genuine care and concern, and providing exceptional service, sales professionals can build trust, loyalty, and advocacy among their clients, fostering enduring relationships that drive sustained sales growth and financial success.

Strategies for client retention and loyalty

There are certain critical strategies for retaining clients and fostering loyalty. Client retention is essential for sustainable business growth, as loyal customers not only contribute to repeat sales but also serve as advocates who can drive referrals and bolster the reputation of your brand. Let's examine the key strategies for maximizing client retention and loyalty:

1. Deliver exceptional customer service.

Exceptional customer service is the bedrock of client retention. Aim to exceed client expectations at every encounter, whether it's during the sales process, product delivery, or ongoing support. Promptly address inquiries, resolve issues, and go the extra mile to ensure client satisfaction.

2. Personalize the customer experience.

Personalization enhances the customer experience and strengthens client relationships. Tailor your communication, recommendations, and offerings to align with each client's preferences, interests, and needs. Use CRM data to personalize interactions and demonstrate that you understand and value your clients as individuals.

3. Provide ongoing value and support.

Continuously provide value to your clients beyond the initial sale. Offer educational resources, industry insights, and exclusive benefits to help clients maximize the value of your products or services. Provide proactive support and guidance to address their evolving needs and challenges.

4. Foster regular communication.

Regular communication is essential for staying top-of-mind with your clients and reinforcing your relationship. Maintain open lines of communication through email newsletters, social media updates, and personalized check-ins. Keep clients informed about new offerings, promotions, and relevant industry news.

5. Solicit and act on feedback.

Soliciting feedback from clients demonstrates that you value their input and are committed to continuous improvement. Regularly seek feedback through surveys, reviews, and one-on-one conversations. Act on feedback to address concerns, make improvements, and show clients that their opinions matter.

6. Offer exclusive rewards and incentives.

Reward client loyalty with exclusive benefits, incentives, and rewards programs. Offer discounts, special offers, or loyalty points for repeat purchases or referrals. Recognize and appreciate loyal clients with personalized gestures, such as handwritten notes or VIP access to events.

7. Build trust and transparency.

Trust is the foundation of long-term client relationships. Build trust by delivering on your promises, being transparent in your communication, and acting with integrity and honesty at all times. Demonstrate reliability, consistency, and accountability in your actions and decisions.

8. Anticipate and address client needs.

Anticipate client needs and proactively offer solutions before they even ask. Stay informed about industry trends, market changes, and emerging challenges that may impact your clients. Offer proactive recommendations, advice, and support to help clients navigate uncertainties and achieve their goals.

9. Stay flexible and adaptive.

Flexibility and adaptability are essential for meeting the evolving needs and expectations of your clients. Be responsive to changing circumstances, preferences, and priorities. Adapt your approach, offerings, and strategies to better align with client goals and preferences over time.

10. Cultivate a Culture of Appreciation

Express gratitude and appreciation for your clients on a regular basis. Acknowledge milestones, anniversaries, and achievements in your client relationships. Celebrate successes together and express genuine appreciation for their loyalty and support.

Handling customer feedback and complaints

Effective handling of customer feedback and complaints is crucial. While every business aims for satisfied customers, it's inevitable that you will encounter feedback, both positive and negative, throughout your interactions. How you respond to this feedback can significantly impact your relationships with customers and, ultimately, your business's success. Here is a list of simple but effective strategies for handling customer feedback and complaints:

1. Active Listening

When a customer provides feedback or lodges a complaint, it's essential to practice active listening. Pay full attention to what the customer is saying without interrupting, and demonstrate empathy and understanding for their perspective. Let the customer know that their feedback is valued and taken seriously.

2. Prompt Response

Respond to customer feedback and complaints promptly. Acknowledge receipt of their message or complaint immediately, even if you need time to investigate or address the issue fully. Timely responses show customers that you prioritize their concerns and are committed to resolving them as quickly as possible.

3. Apologize and empathize.

If a customer expresses dissatisfaction or frustration, offer a sincere apology and empathize with their experience. Acknowledge their feelings and assure them that you understand their concerns. Avoid being nonchalant or dismissive, as this can worsen the situation and further escalate it.

4. Investigate Thoroughly

Take the time to investigate the customer's feedback or complaint thoroughly. Gather all relevant information, including communication records, order history, and any other pertinent details. Understand the root cause of the issue to provide an informed and effective resolution.

5. Provide Solutions

Offer practical and actionable solutions to address the customer's concerns. Propose remedies that aim to resolve the issue satisfactorily and restore the customer's confidence in your business. Be transparent about what steps you will take to rectify the situation and ensure that the customer is satisfied with the outcome.

6. Follow Up

After resolving a customer's complaint or addressing their feedback, follow up with them to ensure their satisfaction. Confirm that the solution provided meets their expectations, and inquire if there's anything else you can do to further assist them. Following up demonstrates your commitment to customer satisfaction and reinforces the value you place on their feedback.

7. Learn and improve.

View customer feedback and complaints as valuable opportunities for learning and improvement. Analyze trends and patterns in feedback to identify areas for enhancement in your products, services, or processes. Use this feedback to implement changes that prevent similar issues from recurring in the future.

8. Empower Employees

Empower your employees to handle customer feedback and complaints effectively. Provide training and guidance on active listening, problem-solving, and conflict resolution techniques. Encourage employees to take ownership of customer issues and empower them to make decisions to resolve them autonomously.

9. Foster a culture of feedback.

Foster a culture within your organization that encourages open communication and feedback from both customers and employees. Create channels for customers to provide feedback easily, such as surveys, suggestion boxes, or dedicated email addresses. Regularly solicit feedback from employees as well, as they often have valuable insights into customer experiences.

10. Monitor and measure

Continuously monitor and measure your handling of customer feedback and complaints. Track metrics such as response time, resolution rate, customer satisfaction scores, and repeat complaints. Use this data to evaluate the effectiveness of your strategies and identify areas for further improvement.

Practical Guide for Developing a Customer Relationship Management Plan

Follow the steps below to create a structured approach to managing customer relationships and maximizing sales opportunities:

1. Define your objectives.

Start by clarifying your objectives for implementing a CRM plan. Identify specific goals related to customer retention, loyalty-building, and feedback management. Determine what outcomes you aim to achieve through your CRM efforts.

2. Assess your current state.

Evaluate your current practices and processes for managing customer relationships. Identify strengths and weaknesses in your approach, as well as any gaps or areas for improvement. Consider factors such as communication channels, data management systems, and customer feedback mechanisms.

3. Segment your customer base.

Segment your customer base based on relevant criteria such as demographics, purchase history, engagement level, and feedback. Group customers into segments with similar characteristics and needs. This segmentation will inform your targeted approach to relationship management.

4. Choose CRM tools and technologies.

Select CRM tools and technologies that align with your objectives and requirements. Consider factors such as functionality, scalability, ease of use, and integration capabilities. Choose a CRM platform that enables you to centralize customer data, automate processes, and track interactions effectively.

5. Develop communication guidelines.

Establish clear guidelines for communication with customers across various channels. Define the frequency, tone, and content of communications, ensuring consistency and relevance. Determine who will be responsible for managing communication and how responses will be coordinated.

6. Implement feedback collection mechanisms.

Set up mechanisms for collecting feedback from customers at various touchpoints. Utilize surveys, feedback forms, social media monitoring, and other tools to gather insights into customer satisfaction, preferences, and concerns. Ensure that feedback collection processes are streamlined and accessible to all customers.

7. Create response protocols.

Develop protocols for handling customer feedback and complaints in a timely and effective manner. Define roles and responsibilities for responding to different types of feedback, including escalation procedures for resolving complex issues. Establish service level agreements (SLAs) for response times and resolution.

8. Train your team.

Provide training to your team members on the importance of CRM as well as the specific strategies and protocols outlined in your CRM plan. Equip them with the skills and knowledge needed to effectively engage with customers, manage relationships, and handle feedback professionally.

9. Monitor and measure performance.

Use KPIs and metrics to monitor the effectiveness of your CRM strategy. Keep an eye on metrics like resolution rates, response times, satisfaction ratings, and client retention rates. To find trends, patterns, and areas that need work, apply data analytics.

10.   Iterate and adapt.

Review and improve your CRM strategy on a regular basis in light of user input and performance metrics. Determine what worked well and what still needs work, then make the necessary changes. Remain flexible and responsive to changing consumer demands and market conditions.

CHAPTER SIX

GROWING YOUR SALES NETWORK AND REFERRAL BUSINESS

Growing your sales network and referral business emphasizes expanding your network of contacts and leveraging referrals to generate new sales opportunities. This involves actively networking, building relationships with industry peers and potential clients, and encouraging satisfied customers to refer others to your business. By continuously expanding your network and cultivating referral sources, you can tap into a steady stream of leads and accelerate your sales growth, ultimately contributing to your financial freedom.

The Power of Networking

There is transformative potential in networking to expand your sales reach and generate valuable referrals. Networking is more than just exchanging business cards at events; it's about building meaningful connections, fostering relationships, and leveraging the collective strength of your network to drive sales growth. Here, we comprehensively delve into the power of networking and its role in maximizing sales opportunities and achieving financial freedom.

1. Expanding Your Reach

Networking opens doors to new opportunities by connecting you with individuals and businesses outside of your immediate circle. By actively engaging in networking events, industry conferences, and online communities, you can expand your reach and access new markets and prospects that may have otherwise been out of reach.

2. Building Trust and Credibility

Building relationships through networking helps establish trust and credibility with potential clients and referral sources. When people know you personally and have interacted with you in professional settings, they are more likely to view you as trustworthy and competent. This trust is invaluable in facilitating sales conversations and securing referrals.

3. Accessing insider knowledge

By networking, you can benefit from the combined experience and wisdom of professionals in your field as well as those of your peers. You can obtain important insights into consumer preferences, market trends, and industry best practices by conversing, exchanging experiences, and asking others in your network for assistance. This will help you make wise decisions and stay one step ahead of the competition.

4. Facilitating collaboration and partnerships

Networking creates opportunities for collaboration and partnerships with complementary businesses and professionals. By connecting with individuals who offer products or services that complement your own, you can explore opportunities for joint ventures, co-marketing initiatives, and referral agreements, expanding your reach and driving mutual business growth.

5. Generating referrals and leads

One of the most powerful aspects of networking is its ability to generate referrals and leads. When you build strong relationships with others in your network and consistently deliver value, they are more likely to refer you to their own contacts who may be in need of your products or services. Referrals from trusted sources carry significant weight and often result in high-quality leads and conversions.

6. Nurturing long-term relationships

Networking is not just about making one-time connections; it's about nurturing long-term relationships that can support your sales efforts over time. By staying in touch with your network, providing value, and offering support when needed, you can cultivate relationships that endure beyond individual transactions, leading to repeat business and ongoing referrals.

7. Overcoming challenges and obstacles

Networking provides a valuable support system that can help you overcome challenges and obstacles in your sales journey. Whether you're facing rejection, encountering objections, or struggling to reach your sales targets, your network can offer encouragement, advice, and practical solutions to help you navigate difficult situations and stay motivated.

8. Continuous learning and growth

Engaging in networking exposes you to diverse perspectives, experiences, and ideas, fostering continuous learning and personal growth. By interacting with individuals from different backgrounds and industries, you can expand your horizons, challenge your assumptions, and develop new skills and insights that contribute to your success as a sales professional.

Cultivating referral partnerships

Referral partnerships involve collaborating with other businesses or professionals who can refer potential clients to you in exchange for reciprocal referrals or other mutual benefits. Cultivating strong referral partnerships can significantly amplify your sales efforts and expand your client base. Below is a thorough guideline for developing referral relationships and optimizing their potential to maximize sales and achieve financial independence:

1. Identify potential partners.

Start by identifying potential referral partners who cater to a similar target market but offer complementary products or services. Look for businesses or professionals whose offerings align with yours and who have a vested interest in helping their clients solve related problems or fulfill additional needs.

2. Establish trust and credibility.

Building trust and credibility is essential to cultivating successful referral partnerships. Take the time to get to know your potential partners, understand their business objectives, and demonstrate how your products or services can add value to their clients. Establishing mutual trust lays the foundation for a fruitful partnership built on collaboration and mutual benefit.

3. Clearly define partnership terms.

Clearly define the terms of your referral partnership to ensure clarity and alignment between both parties. Outline expectations, responsibilities, and incentives for referrals, including how leads will be tracked, rewarded, and followed up on. Having a formal agreement in place helps prevent misunderstandings and ensures a mutually beneficial partnership.

4. Provide value to your partners.

To incentivize your referral partners to send clients your way, provide value to them in return. Offer exclusive discounts, access to resources, or reciprocal referrals to demonstrate your commitment to the partnership. Show appreciation for their referrals and go above and beyond to exceed their expectations.

5. Communicate Effectively

Effective communication is essential for maintaining strong referral partnerships. Keep your partners informed about new offerings, promotions, and updates that may be relevant to their clients. Regularly check in with your partners to assess the effectiveness of the partnership and address any concerns or opportunities for improvement.

6. Track and reward referrals

Implement a system for tracking referrals and rewarding your partners for their efforts. Use CRM tools or referral tracking software to monitor leads generated by each partner and ensure that they receive proper recognition and compensation for their referrals. Recognizing and rewarding successful referrals encourages continued collaboration and engagement.

7. Nurture the relationship.

Like any other relationship, referral partnerships require ongoing nurturing and maintenance. Stay engaged with your partners, offer support when needed, and look for ways to deepen the relationship over time. Show appreciation for their partnership and celebrate shared successes together.

8. Evaluate and optimize

Assess the effectiveness of your referral alliances on a regular basis and look for areas where you can improve. Keep track of important data, including the quantity of referrals you receive, your conversion rates, and the money you make from partner referrals. Utilize this information to pinpoint high-achieving collaborators, enhance your collaboration approach, and investigate novel partnership prospects.

9. Expand your network.

Continuously seek out new referral partners to expand your network and reach new audiences. Attend networking events, join industry associations, and leverage online platforms to connect with potential partners who align with your business objectives. The more diverse and extensive your network of referral partners, the greater your potential for sales growth.

10. Foster a culture of collaboration.

Encourage cooperation and teamwork among employees in your company. As part of their sales efforts, encourage team members to proactively seek out and nurture referral partnerships. Acknowledge and thank staff members who make referral partnerships successful, emphasizing the value of teamwork in maximizing sales.

Strategies for Expanding Your Sales Network

Understanding and implementing effective strategies for expanding your sales network is crucial. Expanding your network allows you to connect with new prospects, build relationships with industry peers, and uncover valuable sales opportunities. Implement the following strategies in order to expand your sales network:

1. Attend networking events.

Networking events provide valuable opportunities to connect with professionals from diverse industries and backgrounds. Attend industry conferences, trade shows, seminars, and local business networking events to expand your network and engage with potential clients and referral sources.

2. Join professional associations.

Joining professional associations and industry-specific organizations can help you establish credibility within your field and connect with like-minded professionals. Participate in association events, committees, and forums to network with peers, share insights, and stay informed about industry trends and developments.

3. Leverage online platforms.

Utilize online platforms such as LinkedIn, Twitter, and industry-specific forums to expand your professional network beyond geographical boundaries. Join relevant groups and communities, participate in discussions, and engage with potential prospects and influencers in your industry.

4. Host workshops and seminars.

Hosting workshops, seminars, or webinars on topics relevant to your industry or target market can attract new prospects and position you as an authority in your field. Invite industry professionals, clients, and prospects to attend, and use these events as opportunities to network and build relationships.

5. Volunteer and give back.

Volunteering for industry associations, charitable organizations, or community events not only allows you to give back to your community but also presents networking opportunities. Volunteering can help you connect with like-minded individuals who share your values and interests, leading to valuable professional connections.

6. Cultivate Online Presence

Build a strong online presence through your website, blog, and social media channels to attract and engage potential clients and referral partners. Share valuable content, insights, and resources that demonstrate your expertise and provide value to your audience, attracting followers and opportunities for engagement.

7. Utilize referral programs.

Implement referral programs that incentivize existing clients, partners, and contacts to refer new business to you. Offer rewards, discounts, or exclusive benefits for successful referrals, encouraging individuals in your network to actively promote your products or services to their connections.

8. Establish strategic partnerships.

Identify businesses or professionals whose offerings complement yours and explore opportunities for strategic partnerships. Collaborate on joint ventures, co-marketing campaigns, or bundled offerings that provide mutual value to both parties and allow you to tap into each other's networks.

9. Attend social gatherings.

Attend social gatherings, community events, and networking mixers to meet new people outside of formal business settings. Building relationships in a more relaxed environment can lead to genuine connections and valuable business opportunities.

10.   Follow up and nurture relationships.

After making new connections, be proactive about following up and nurturing relationships over time. Stay in touch with your contacts through personalized emails, LinkedIn messages, or occasional phone calls. Continuously provide value and seek opportunities to collaborate with or assist them in achieving their goals.

Practical Guide for Networking Action Plan

To help you take concrete steps to improve your networking and propel sales development toward financial independence, refer to the helpful information below.

1. Define your networking goals.

Start by clearly defining your networking goals based on the insights gained from understanding the power of networking. Determine what you aim to achieve through your networking efforts, whether it's expanding your client base, generating referrals, or building strategic partnerships.

2. Identify target networks and events.

Identify the networks, events, and communities where your target audience and potential referral partners are likely to gather. Research industry conferences, networking events, professional associations, and online platforms that align with your objectives.

3. Develop your elevator pitch.

Craft a concise and compelling elevator pitch that effectively communicates who you are, what you do, and the value you provide to your audience. Practice delivering your elevator pitch until it becomes natural and engaging, allowing you to make a memorable impression when networking.

4. Prepare networking materials.

Prepare professional networking materials, including business cards, brochures, and other promotional materials that showcase your brand and offerings. Ensure that your materials are visually appealing, informative, and consistent with your brand identity.

5. Attend networking events regularly.

Commit to attending networking events regularly as part of your networking action plan. Schedule time in your calendar to attend industry conferences, seminars, workshops, and local business networking events where you can connect with potential clients and referral partners.

6. Engage in meaningful conversations.

When networking, focus on engaging in meaningful conversations with other attendees rather than simply exchanging business cards. Listen actively, ask thoughtful questions, and demonstrate genuine interest in learning about others' businesses and challenges.

7. Nurture referral partnerships.

Identify potential referral partners and initiate conversations to explore collaboration opportunities. Communicate the value of a referral partnership and how it can benefit both parties. Be proactive in providing referrals to your partners and reciprocate their gestures of goodwill.

8. Leverage online networking platforms.

Utilize online networking platforms such as LinkedIn, industry forums, and social media groups to expand your professional network beyond geographical boundaries. Engage in relevant discussions, share valuable insights, and connect with potential clients and partners.

9. Follow up and stay connected.

After networking events, follow up with individuals you've met to express appreciation for the conversation and continue building the relationship. Send personalized follow-up emails, connect on LinkedIn, and schedule follow-up meetings or calls to explore potential collaboration further.

10. Evaluate and adjust your approach.

Regularly evaluate the effectiveness of your networking efforts and adjust your approach as needed. Track key metrics such as the number of new connections made, referrals generated, and business opportunities identified. Use this feedback to refine your networking action plan and optimize your future networking activities.

CHAPTER SEVEN

NAVIGATING THE SALES PROCESS IN VARIOUS INDUSTRIES

Navigating the sales process in various industries explores the intricacies of selling across different sectors, highlighting the unique challenges and strategies involved in each industry. This chapter provides insights into adapting sales techniques, understanding industry-specific trends, and addressing the needs of diverse clientele. By mastering the nuances of the sales process across various industries, readers can tailor their approach effectively and maximize their success in any market.

Selling in B2B vs. B2C Environments

It's crucial to comprehensively understand the distinctions between selling in business-to-business (B2B) and business-to-consumer (B2C) environments. Both B2B and B2C sales involve unique dynamics, customer behaviors, and strategies. Let's delve into a thorough exploration of selling in these two distinct environments:

Understanding B2B Sales

Target Audience: B2B sales concentrate on offering goods and services to other companies as opposed to private customers. Professionals, decision-makers, and procurement teams working for organizations make up the target audience.

Longer Sales Cycles: B2B sales typically involve longer and more complex sales cycles compared to B2C sales. Decision-making in B2B environments often requires consensus among multiple stakeholders and a thorough evaluation of ROI.

Relationship-driven: B2B sales are highly relationship-driven, emphasizing trust, credibility, and ongoing collaboration. Building long-term partnerships with clients is essential for success in B2B sales.

Value Proposition: B2B sales revolve around offering solutions that address specific business needs, pain points, and objectives. Sales pitches should focus on demonstrating the value and ROI of the product or service to the business as a whole.

Key Strategies for B2B Sales

Targeted Prospecting: Identify and target businesses that align with your ideal customer profile and have a genuine need for your offerings. Utilize account-based marketing (ABM) strategies to personalize your approach and engage key decision-makers.

Consultative Selling: Take a consultative approach to B2B sales, paying particular attention to comprehending the individual needs and objectives of each customer. Present yourself as a reliable resource with the ability to offer specialized solutions to meet their unique needs.

Building Relationships: Invest time and effort in building strong relationships with key stakeholders within client organizations. Regular communication, personalized interactions, and delivering exceptional service are crucial for fostering trust and loyalty.

Demonstrating Value: Clearly articulate the value proposition of your products or services and demonstrate how they can drive tangible outcomes and ROI for the client's business. Provide case studies, testimonials, and data-driven insights to support your claims.

Understanding B2C Sales

Target Audience: B2C sales target individual consumers, focusing on meeting their personal needs, preferences, and desires. The target audience includes individuals shopping for personal use or consumption.

Shorter Sales Cycles: B2C sales typically have shorter and more straightforward sales cycles compared to B2B sales. Purchase decisions are often influenced by emotions, impulses, and immediate needs.

Brand Perception: B2C sales heavily rely on brand perception, marketing, and emotional appeal to capture consumers' attention and drive purchasing decisions. Building brand loyalty and trust is essential for success in B2C sales.

Convenience and Experience: B2C sales prioritize convenience, seamless shopping experiences, and personalized interactions to enhance customer satisfaction and loyalty.

Key Strategies for B2C Sales

Emotional Appeal: Appeal to consumers' emotions, aspirations, and desires through compelling storytelling, visual imagery, and engaging content. Create memorable experiences that resonate with consumers on a personal level.

Omni-channel Presence: Establish a strong omni-channel presence across multiple platforms and channels to reach consumers wherever they are and provide a seamless shopping experience. Leverage e-commerce platforms, social media, mobile apps, and brick-and-mortar stores to maximize accessibility.

Customer Engagement: Foster ongoing engagement with consumers through personalized communications, loyalty programs, and post-purchase support. Encourage customer reviews, feedback, and user-generated content to build social proof and trust.

Upselling and cross-selling Utilize upselling and cross-selling techniques to increase average order value and maximize revenue per customer. Recommend complementary products or upgrades based on the consumer's preferences and purchase history.

Adapting sales techniques

Tailored Approach: Adapt your sales techniques and messaging to suit the specific needs, preferences, and behaviors of the target audience in B2B and B2C environments. Customize your approach based on factors such as industry norms, buyer personas, and purchase motivations.

Communication Style: Adjust your communication style and tone to resonate with the professional language and expectations of B2B clients or the more casual and conversational tone of B2C consumers.

Sales Channels: Choose the most effective sales channels and touchpoints to reach your target audience in each environment. While B2B sales may rely more on direct sales teams, industry events, and targeted marketing campaigns, B2C sales may leverage e-commerce platforms, social media advertising, and influencer partnerships.

Integrating Technology

CRM Systems: Implement Customer Relationship Management (CRM) systems to manage and track interactions with clients and prospects in both B2B and B2C environments. Utilize CRM data to personalize communications, forecast sales, and identify opportunities for upselling or cross-selling.

Marketing Automation: Leverage marketing automation tools to streamline lead generation, nurture campaigns, and customer engagement efforts in both B2B and B2C sales. Automate repetitive tasks, such as email follow-ups and social media scheduling, to save time and improve efficiency.

In a nutshell, understanding the nuances of selling in B2B vs. B2C environments is essential for navigating the sales process effectively across various industries. By recognizing the distinct characteristics, customer behaviors, and strategies involved in each environment, sales professionals can tailor their approach, adapt their techniques, and maximize their success in driving sales and achieving financial freedom.

Understanding Industry-Specific Challenges

It's essential to comprehensively understand the industry-specific challenges that sales professionals may encounter. Each industry presents unique dynamics, trends, and obstacles that can impact the sales process. By gaining insights into these challenges, sales professionals can tailor their strategies, overcome barriers, and maximize their success. Some of these challenges are:

1. Market Dynamics

Different industries operate within distinct market dynamics characterized by factors such as demand fluctuations, the competitive landscape, regulatory requirements, and technological advancements. Sales professionals must stay abreast of industry trends, market shifts, and emerging opportunities to effectively navigate these dynamics.

2. Customer needs and preferences

Each industry caters to specific customer needs, preferences, and pain points. Understanding the unique challenges and priorities of customers within a particular industry is crucial for aligning sales strategies and positioning products or services effectively. Sales professionals must conduct thorough market research and customer analysis to identify and address these needs.

3. Competitive Landscape

The competitive landscape varies across industries, with different players vying for market share and customer attention. Sales professionals must assess competitors' strengths, weaknesses, and strategies to differentiate their offerings and effectively position them in the market. Understanding competitive pricing, product features, and value propositions is essential for success.

4. Industry Regulations and Compliance

Many industries are subject to regulatory requirements, compliance standards, and industry-specific regulations governing product sales and marketing practices. Sales professionals must navigate these regulations ethically and ensure compliance to avoid legal issues or reputational damage. Maintaining up-to-date knowledge of industry regulations and seeking legal guidance when necessary is imperative.

5. Technological Disruption

Technological advancements and digital disruption impact various industries, revolutionizing business processes, customer expectations, and sales strategies. Sales professionals must embrace technology-enabled sales tools, automation platforms, and data analytics to stay competitive and enhance productivity. Adapting to technological changes and leveraging innovative solutions can drive sales growth and customer engagement.

6. Economic Factors

Economic factors such as market volatility, inflation, interest rates, and geopolitical events can significantly influence buying behavior and purchasing decisions across industries. Sales professionals must anticipate and adapt to economic fluctuations, tailor pricing strategies, and offer flexible payment options to mitigate risks and capitalize on opportunities.

7. Industry-Specific Challenges

Each industry presents its own unique set of challenges that sales professionals must navigate. For example:

In the healthcare industry, sales professionals may encounter stringent regulations, complex procurement processes, and resistance to change from healthcare providers.

In the technology sector, sales professionals may face rapid technological advancements, evolving customer preferences, and intense competition from innovative startups.

In the manufacturing sector, sales professionals may grapple with global supply chain disruptions, fluctuating raw material prices, and the need to demonstrate ROI to risk-averse stakeholders.

8. Cultural and regional differences

Cultural nuances and regional differences can influence sales dynamics and customer behavior across different markets. Sales professionals operating in diverse regions must adapt their communication styles, sales approaches, and marketing strategies to resonate with local customs, preferences, and business practices.

9. Client Relationship Management

Building and maintaining relationships with clients within specific industries requires an understanding of industry-specific challenges and pain points. Sales professionals must demonstrate empathy, industry knowledge, and tailored solutions to earn trust, address concerns, and foster long-term partnerships.

10. Continuous learning and adaptation

Successfully navigating industry-specific challenges requires a commitment to continuous learning, adaptation, and professional development. Sales professionals must stay informed about industry trends, attend industry conferences, participate in relevant training programs, and seek mentorship to refine their skills and stay ahead of the curve.

Adapting Sales Strategies to Different Niches

Understanding how to adapt sales strategies to different niches is essential for sales professionals aiming to achieve financial freedom through sales maximization. Each niche market comes with its own unique set of characteristics, customer behaviors, and challenges, necessitating tailored approaches to effectively engage and convert prospects. Let's explore different strategies for adapting sales techniques across different niches:

1. Market research and segmentation

Begin by conducting thorough market research to identify niche markets within your industry. Segment these markets based on factors such as demographics, psychographics, purchasing behaviors, and pain points. Understanding the specific needs and preferences of each niche segment is crucial for tailoring your sales strategies effectively.

2. Customized Value Proposition

Develop a customized value proposition tailored to address the unique needs and challenges of each niche market. Highlight how your product or service solves specific problems or fulfills distinct desires within each niche segment. Communicate the value proposition in a way that resonates with the target audience's motivations and priorities.

3. Targeted messaging and positioning

Craft targeted messaging and positioning strategies that speak directly to the pain points, aspirations, and interests of each niche market. Tailor your sales pitch, marketing materials, and communication channels to align with the preferences and communication styles prevalent within each niche segment. Speak the language of your audience to establish rapport and credibility.

4. Industry-Specific Expertise

Develop industry-specific expertise and knowledge relevant to each niche market you target. Position yourself as a trusted advisor who understands the unique challenges and opportunities within the niche and can provide valuable insights and solutions. Demonstrate your expertise through thought leadership content, case studies, and client testimonials.

5. Flexible Sales Approaches

Adopt flexible sales approaches that accommodate the varied buying preferences and decision-making processes prevalent across different niche markets. Some niches may respond well to consultative selling techniques, while others may prefer a more transactional approach. Be adaptable and responsive to the unique dynamics of each niche segment.

6. Personalized customer experiences

Prioritize personalized customer experiences tailored to the needs and preferences of each niche market. Customize your interactions, product recommendations, and follow-up communications to reflect the specific requirements and preferences of individual customers within each niche segment. Demonstrate that you understand their unique challenges and are committed to delivering solutions that meet their needs.

7. Relationship building and trust

Invest time and effort in building relationships and fostering trust within each niche market. Engage with niche-specific communities, forums, and events where your target audience congregates. Demonstrate authenticity, transparency, and integrity in your interactions to establish trust and credibility within each niche segment.

8. Continuous Optimization and Adaptation

Continuously monitor and analyze the performance of your sales strategies within each niche market. Gather feedback from customers, track key metrics, and adapt your approach based on insights gained. Be open to experimenting with new tactics and refining your strategies to better resonate with the evolving needs of each niche segment.

9. Leverage technology and data

Utilize technology and data-driven insights to enhance your sales efforts within different niche markets. Leverage customer relationship management (CRM) systems, analytics tools, and automation platforms to segment your audience, personalize your communications, and track the effectiveness of your sales strategies. Harness the power of data to make informed decisions and optimize your approach over time.

10. Collaborate and partner

Explore opportunities for collaboration and partnership within each niche market to extend your reach and credibility. Identify complementary businesses or influencers within the niche and explore mutually beneficial partnerships. Collaborate on joint marketing campaigns, co-branded initiatives, or referral programs to leverage each other's networks and resources.

Practical Guide for Industry-Specific Sales Strategies

We have outlined actionable steps for developing industry-specific sales strategies to effectively navigate various environments, including B2B and B2C, understanding industry-specific challenges, and adapting sales techniques to different niches in the practical guide below. By following these steps, readers can internalize key concepts and implement tailored sales approaches to achieve success in diverse markets.

1. Research and understand your target industry.

Begin by conducting comprehensive research to understand the dynamics, trends, and challenges within your target industry. Explore industry publications, reports, and online resources to gain insights into market conditions, customer preferences, and the competitive landscape.

2. Identify industry-specific challenges and opportunities.

Analyze the unique challenges and opportunities inherent in the target industry. Consider factors such as regulatory requirements, technological advancements, economic trends, and customer needs. Identify areas where your products or services can address industry-specific pain points and add value to customers.

3. Tailor Your Approach for B2B vs. B2C Environments

Recognize the differences between B2B and B2C sales environments and tailor your approach accordingly. For B2B sales, focus on building relationships, demonstrating ROI, and addressing the business needs of corporate clients. For B2C sales, emphasize emotional appeal, convenience, and personalized experiences to engage individual consumers effectively.

4. Develop industry-specific value propositions.

Craft compelling value propositions that resonate with the specific needs and priorities of your target industry. Highlight how your products or services solve industry-specific challenges, improve efficiency, reduce costs, or drive growth. Tailor your messaging to showcase the unique benefits and advantages relevant to each industry segment.

5. Customize sales techniques for different niches.

Segment your target audience into distinct niches based on demographics, psychographics, and purchasing behaviors. Develop customized sales techniques and messaging strategies for each niche, addressing their unique pain points and preferences. Personalize your approach to build rapport and establish credibility within each niche market.

6. Leverage industry-specific expertise.

Cultivate industry-specific expertise and knowledge to position yourself as a trusted advisor within your target industry. Stay updated on industry trends, regulations, and best practices to provide valuable insights and recommendations to clients. Demonstrate your understanding of industry-specific challenges and solutions during sales interactions.

7. Build relationships and networks within the industry.

Devote time and energy to creating networks and connections within the intended industry. To establish connections with influential people, decision-makers, and important stakeholders, attend conferences, networking events, and industry events. Take part in insightful discussions, exchange ideas, and make a name for yourself in business as a useful resource.

8. Test and iterate your sales strategies.

Continuously test and iterate your sales strategies to optimize performance and adapt to changing market dynamics. Collect feedback from clients, analyze sales data, and monitor the effectiveness of your approaches.

Experiment with different tactics, messages, and channels to identify what resonates best with your target audience.

9. Stay flexible and agile in your approach.

Keep your sales strategy adaptable and flexible to take into account changing consumer preferences and market developments. To stay ahead of the competition, be receptive to criticism, make necessary adjustments to your tactics, and value innovation. Quickly adjust to shifting market conditions and take advantage of expansion prospects.

10. Measure success and refine your strategies.

Define key performance indicators (KPIs) to measure the success of your industry-specific sales strategies. Track metrics such as conversion rates, customer acquisition costs, and customer satisfaction scores to evaluate performance. Use data-driven insights to refine your strategies, allocate resources effectively, and drive continuous improvement.

CHAPTER EIGHT

CONTINUOUS LEARNING AND IMPROVEMENT IN SALES

The need for continuing professional growth and honing sales techniques is emphasized by continuous learning and improvement in sales as a means of achieving long-term success in the field. It emphasizes how important it is for salespeople to be abreast of changes in the market, in consumer behavior, and in developing technologies. Salespeople may adjust their strategies, hone their craft, and maintain an advantage over rivals by constantly learning and seeking feedback. In order to achieve financial freedom, this chapter highlights a growth mentality, a dedication to self-improvement, and exceptional sales performance.

The importance of ongoing training and education

When it comes to achieving financial independence through sales maximization, sales professionals must never stop learning and growing. Ongoing education not only improves sales abilities but also promotes professional and personal development, allowing people to thrive in their jobs and adjust to changing market conditions. Let's examine the overall significance of continuing education and training in sales:

- Keeping Pace with Industry Trends

The business landscape is constantly evolving, with new technologies, market trends, and consumer behaviors shaping the sales environment. Ongoing training and education allow sales professionals to stay updated with industry trends, emerging technologies, and best practices, enabling them to remain competitive and relevant in their respective fields.

- Adapting to changing customer needs

Customer preferences and needs are subject to change due to various factors, such as economic conditions, technological advancements, and cultural shifts. Ongoing training equips sales professionals with the knowledge and skills needed to adapt to changing customer needs, anticipate market shifts, and tailor their sales approaches accordingly to better meet customer expectations.

- Enhancing sales skills and techniques

Sales is both an art and a science, requiring a diverse set of skills and techniques to engage prospects, overcome objections, and close deals effectively. Continuous training and education provide opportunities for sales professionals to hone their sales skills, such as active listening, negotiation, persuasion, and relationship-building, leading to improved sales performance and higher conversion rates.

- Embracing innovation and technology

The advent of new technologies and tools has revolutionized the sales process, offering innovative solutions for prospecting, lead generation, and customer relationship management. Ongoing training helps sales professionals stay abreast of the latest technological advancements, such as CRM systems, sales automation tools, and data analytics platforms, empowering them to leverage these tools effectively to streamline their sales processes and enhance productivity.

- Fostering personal and professional growth

Continuous learning goes beyond acquiring technical skills; it fosters personal and professional growth by expanding knowledge, building confidence, and nurturing a growth mindset. Sales professionals who invest in ongoing training and education develop a sense of self-improvement and self-motivation, leading to greater job satisfaction, career advancement, and overall fulfillment.

- Building Credibility and Trust

Sales professionals who demonstrate a commitment to ongoing learning and improvement are viewed as credible and trustworthy partners by clients and prospects. Continuous training enhances sales professionals' knowledge base and expertise, instilling confidence in their ability to deliver value and solve customers' problems effectively, thereby strengthening client relationships and fostering long-term loyalty.

- Remaining Resilient in the Face of Challenges

The sales industry is notoriously difficult, as salespeople frequently encounter failures, rejections, and resistance. By providing them with the mentality and abilities necessary to overcome obstacles, learn from mistakes, and keep pushing after their objectives, ongoing training aids in the development of resilience and perseverance in sales professionals.

- Cultivating a Culture of Learning and Collaboration

Organizations that prioritize ongoing training and education create a culture of learning and collaboration where employees are encouraged to share knowledge, insights, and best practices. Sales teams benefit from collective learning experiences, peer-to-peer mentoring, and collaborative problem-solving, leading to a more cohesive and high-performing sales organization.

- Adapting to a Remote and Digital Sales Environment

The rise of remote work and digital sales environments necessitates a shift in sales strategies and techniques. Ongoing training equips sales professionals with the skills needed to thrive in virtual selling environments, such as effective communication through digital channels, virtual relationship-building, and leveraging technology for remote collaboration and sales presentations.

- Driving business growth and financial success

Ultimately, ongoing training and education in sales play a crucial role in driving business growth and financial success. Sales professionals who invest in continuous learning are better equipped to achieve their sales targets, exceed revenue goals, and contribute to the overall success of their organizations, leading to greater financial rewards and opportunities for advancement.

Staying updated with industry trends and innovations

It is imperative for sales professionals who aim to achieve financial independence through sales maximization to be abreast of industry changes and advances. Keeping up with industry trends, new technologies, and creative sales techniques is crucial for sustaining a competitive edge and boosting sales in today's quickly changing business environment. Let's look at the importance of being up-to-date with changes and patterns in the industry at large.

- Anticipating Market Shifts and Opportunities

Sales professionals who keep up with industry trends are better able to predict changes in the market and spot new chances before they become popular. Sales professionals may position themselves and their offerings ahead of the curve, earning a first-mover advantage and winning market share in new and developing categories, by knowing where the market is headed.

- Identifying customer needs and preferences

Shifts in consumer demands, tastes, and habits are frequently reflected in industry trends. Sales professionals can learn about changing consumer expectations, pain spots, and purchasing behaviors by keeping up with industry trends. Equipped with this understanding, businesses may adjust their language, product offers, and sales strategies to more closely match the expectations of their target audience, improving their chances of success.

- Enhancing product knowledge and expertise

Industry trends often coincide with innovations and advancements in products, services, and solutions. Sales professionals who stay updated with industry trends are better equipped to understand and communicate the value proposition of their offerings effectively. By staying informed about new features, functionalities, and benefits, sales professionals can enhance their product knowledge and position themselves as trusted advisors to their clients.

- Leveraging emerging technologies

New tools and technology that have the potential to completely transform the sales process are frequently adopted due to industry developments. By keeping abreast of industry developments, sales professionals may take advantage of cutting-edge technologies like automation, machine learning, artificial intelligence, and data analytics to improve client experiences, expedite sales processes, and obtain a competitive edge in the market.

- Differentiating from competitors

By providing their clients with cutting-edge solutions and insights, sales professionals may set themselves apart from rivals by remaining abreast of industry trends. Sales professionals may differentiate themselves from the competition by being at the forefront of industry trends and breakthroughs. This allows them to position themselves as trusted advisors and thought leaders who can provide their clients with insightful advice and recommendations.

- Adapting sales strategies and approaches

Industry trends often require sales professionals to adapt their sales strategies and approaches to remain relevant and effective. By staying updated with industry trends, sales professionals can identify shifts in buyer behavior, market dynamics, and the competitive landscape, allowing them to adjust their sales strategies accordingly. Whether it's adopting new sales techniques, embracing digital selling channels, or refining their value proposition, staying informed enables sales professionals to stay ahead of the curve and drive success in sales.

- Networking and building relationships

Keeping up with market trends gives salespeople excellent networking chances to meet thought leaders, potential customers, and industry experts. Sales professionals can develop lasting relationships with important industry players, share insights, and broaden their professional network by taking part in conferences, events, and online forums.

- Demonstrating industry knowledge and credibility

Salespeople who keep up with industry developments show that they are dedicated to lifelong learning and industry expertise. With this, sales professionals may establish their expertise in their field and project credibility by keeping up to date with the latest developments, trends, and best practices in the industry. Customers are more willing to interact with salespeople who are knowledgeable about their sector and can offer insightful advice when they are credible and trustworthy.

- Navigating Regulatory Changes and Compliance

Industry trends often coincide with changes in regulations, compliance standards, and industry practices. Sales professionals who stay updated with industry trends can navigate regulatory changes effectively, ensuring that their sales practices remain compliant with industry regulations and standards. By staying informed about regulatory developments, sales professionals can mitigate risks and avoid potential legal issues that could impact their sales efforts.

- Driving innovation and continuous improvement

Lastly, being abreast of market developments encourages a continuous innovation and improvement mindset in sales companies. Organizations can promote innovation in sales processes, goods, and services by motivating sales personnel to remain inquisitive, investigate novel concepts, and welcome modifications. This proactive approach to keeping abreast of market developments guarantees that salespeople are constantly seeking methods to innovate and enhance their work, which promotes long-term success and financial independence in the sales sector.

Practical Guide for Creating a Personal Development Plan for Sales Success

In this helpful guide, we'll walk you through the process of developing a personal development plan that will help you improve your sales abilities, gain knowledge from your experiences, and keep up with industry trends.

You can increase your chances of success and financial independence in sales by completing these stages within the allotted time.

- Define Your Goals and Objectives (Week 1)

Spend some time defining your personal development goals and objectives in sales. Think about the particular abilities you wish to develop, the information you wish to acquire, and the way you see yourself succeeding in sales. Put your objectives down in writing, making sure they are SMART (specific, measurable, attainable, relevant, and time-bound).

- Assess Your Current Skills and Knowledge (Week 2)

Conduct a thorough self-assessment to identify your current strengths and weaknesses in sales. Reflect on past experiences, successes, and failures to gain insights into areas for improvement. Consider seeking feedback from mentors, colleagues, or supervisors to gain a comprehensive understanding of your skillset.

- Research Ongoing Training Opportunities (Week 3)

Research and identify ongoing training opportunities that align with your personal development goals. Look for workshops, courses, webinars, or conferences focused on sales skills, techniques, and industry trends. Consider online resources, professional associations, and reputable training providers to find relevant learning opportunities.

- Develop a Learning Schedule (Week 4)

Create a learning schedule that outlines how you'll allocate time for ongoing training and education. Determine how many hours per week you'll dedicate to learning activities and block off specific time slots in your calendar. Be consistent and disciplined in following your learning schedule to maximize your progress.

- Learn from Failures and Successes (Weeks 5–6)

Reflect on past failures and successes in sales to extract valuable lessons and insights. Analyze what went well in successful sales interactions and what could have been improved in unsuccessful ones. Use these learnings to inform your personal development plan and set specific goals for improvement.

- Stay updated with industry trends (weeks 7-8).

Stay informed about industry trends, innovations, and best practices relevant to your sales role. Follow industry news, subscribe to relevant publications, and engage with thought leaders on social media platforms. Dedicate time each week to staying updated on the latest developments in your industry.

- Networking and Mentorship (Weeks 9–10)

Build relationships with peers, mentors, and industry experts who can provide guidance and support in your sales journey. Attend networking events, join professional associations, and seek out mentorship opportunities to expand your network and gain valuable insights from experienced professionals.

- Implement Continuous Improvement Strategies (Weeks 11–12)

Implement strategies for continuous improvement by setting actionable goals and tracking your progress regularly. Review your personal development plan, assess your performance, and adjust your strategies as needed. Stay proactive in seeking out learning opportunities and applying new skills and knowledge to your sales activities.

- Monitor Your Progress (Weeks 13–14)

Monitor your progress towards your personal development goals by tracking key performance indicators (KPIs) and milestones. Keep a journal or use a goal-tracking app to document your achievements, challenges, and lessons learned along the way. Review your progress regularly to stay on track and motivated.

- Review and Adjust Your Plan (Week 15)

At the conclusion of the allotted time, review your personal growth plan and evaluate your overall performance. Honor your accomplishments and pinpoint areas in which you still need to grow. As opportunities arise, circumstances change, and you receive input from mentors or peers, make the necessary adjustments to your plan.

You can construct a customized development plan for sales success in 15 weeks if you adhere to this practical guidance and set aside time each week to complete the stages. Maintaining your focus, embracing lifelong learning, and always seeking better are the keys to achieving financial independence through sales maximization.

CONCLUSION

As we conclude our journey through "How to Sell Anything to Anyone: A Step-by-Step Guide to Financial Freedom Through Sales Maximization," it's essential to reflect on the transformative power of sales mastery. Throughout this comprehensive guide, we've explored the intricacies of the sales process, from mastering the mindset of a successful salesperson to leveraging technology and social media, and from building long-term relationships to navigating diverse industry landscapes.

At its core, this book is more than just a collection of techniques and strategies; it's a blueprint for unlocking your full potential and achieving financial freedom. By understanding the psychology of selling and overcoming limiting beliefs, you've laid the groundwork for success. By honing your product knowledge and developing effective sales techniques, you've equipped yourself with the tools to thrive in any sales environment. By embracing continuous learning and improvement, you've positioned yourself as a dynamic force in the world of sales.

But beyond the practical skills and strategies, this book is about empowerment. It's about realizing that the ability to sell is not just reserved for a select few but rather a skill that can be learned, honed, and mastered by anyone willing to put in the effort. It's about recognizing that financial freedom is not a distant dream but a tangible reality within your grasp.

As you close the final pages of this guide, I encourage you to carry forward the lessons learned and apply them with diligence and determination. Whether you're a seasoned sales professional or just starting on your journey, remember that every interaction presents an opportunity to make a difference, to add value, and to move closer to your goals.

In essence, "How to Sell Anything to Anyone" is not merely a manual for sales proficiency; it is a roadmap to financial freedom. By embracing the principles outlined within these pages and committing to continuous learning and improvement, readers have the opportunity to chart their course towards unparalleled success in the realm of sales. May this guide serve as a beacon of inspiration and empowerment as you embark on your journey to sales mastery and financial abundance.

So go forth with confidence, knowing that you possess the knowledge, skills, and mindset to sell anything to anyone. May this book serve as a constant companion and source of inspiration as you embark on your path to financial freedom through sales maximization. The world is yours for the taking—now go out there and seize it.